SCOOP IT CHOP IT COOK IT

 **MY COOKING HOUSE RULES**

1. Each Recipe Should Take No More than 15 Minutes of Prep Time
2. Each Recipe Should Take No More than 15 Minutes of Cleaning Time
3. Each Recipe Should Have 7 or Fewer Ingredients
4. Each Recipe Should Have 7 or Fewer Steps

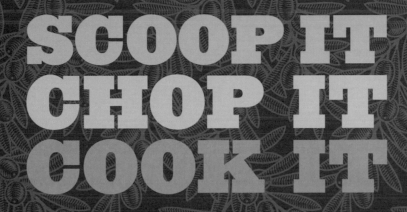

SCOOP IT CHOP IT COOK IT

Easy Family Feasts from Your
Mediterranean Bar

Tara Brennan

PHOTOGRAPHY BY
Joshua Shaub

FEAST BOOKS

Contents

Introduction

IT'S 5:30 PM AND YOU'RE WANDERING THE AISLES OF YOUR local supermarket, wondering what to fix for dinner, quickly, but without eating out of a can or box. Pasta or chicken come to mind, but who has time to clean the vegetables and prep the sauce? Amazingly, you'll find many of the ingredients for your meal, fresh and already seasoned, in your local supermarket's Mediterranean bar (I call it the MedBar), or perhaps in the deli case. The Mediterranean bar is often viewed as a place for cold appetizers, but rarely is it recognized that the MedBar has dozens of ready-made vegetables marinated in oil and vinegar that can be used as ingredients for seemingly elaborate meals in minutes. You've struck gold when you see a variety of olives—Kalamata, Castelvetrano, picholine—as well as roasted tomatoes, cipolline onions, roasted peppers, Peppadew, and other colorful items displayed side by side on a MedBar, ready for scooping, or in bowls behind the glass in the deli case.

The pages and recipes in this book present delicious, simple dishes that rely on MedBar ingredients to do the heavy culinary lifting for you. You will learn how to use a range of antipasti to add color and depth to your cooking, all the while shaving items off your shopping list and steps off your prep work and cooking time.

All the MedBar offerings are delicious as stand-alone items, served in a bowl alongside cheeses and sliced bread. In fact, the term "antipasto bar" is often used for the MedBar, referring to the Italian word *antipasto*, which means "before the meal."

That said, the magic happens when we consider these products as more than simply antipasti. What if we start to think about them as the base for sauces or salads? As pasta toppings? As versatile, viable ingredients? My recipes take advantage of the fact that most items you find on the MedBar are presented in a bath of brine or light vinaigrette. Some are spiced in the style of a particular country or region; others rely on a light dressing to express provenance.

In using the MedBar approach to cooking, you will work with all-natural products. You will embrace the classic flavors of the Mediterranean. You will develop your own ideas, and you will run with them.

Introducing Me

For years, working in the food business, I've traveled to the Mediterranean region—Italy, Greece, France—always enjoying the slow pace of life and the focus on food and eating. Most often when eating out, I appreciate casual places that serve antipasti: grilled, marinated, or brined vegetables laid out with cheese and prosciutto. A spoonful of marinated artichokes with feta, a hearty chunk of bread…for me, that's the perfect start to a meal.

It wasn't always this way: As an American woman born in the 1970s, I fall into the common category of those raised on mediocre food of low nutritional value, and on most evenings we ate meat loaf or hot dogs. Well before I was born, my grandmother remarried a wonderful Italian man who owned a restaurant and had an exceptional ability to prepare simple, delicious meals; he also clearly loved doing it. Spending long periods of time with him during the summer had a great impact on me, and at a very young age I decided I wanted to be in the food business.

As a late teen I worked for a wholesale bakery, then a smoked fish factory, and later a specialty distributor that supplied restaurants. These work experiences have always required me to genuinely recognize and speak to the details and nuances of why a particular food is special.

Currently, as vice president at a company that produces and imports authentic Mediterranean foods, I eat delicious, naturally prepared olives and antipasti from around the world every day. I am fortunate to have such an amazing job: For almost twenty years I've been talking

about my products, conducting training sessions in great supermarkets and gourmet stores around the country for people who love food. I talk to restaurant chefs about why, perhaps, my ingredients are as good as what they could make themselves in their own kitchens. I also travel to working farms worldwide and meet the people who devote themselves to producing luscious olives, tomatoes, onions, beans, peppers, and artichokes.

Several years ago, while pregnant with my daughter, I had an epiphany. I was traveling a lot and trying to eat as healthily as possible; as the months went by, I felt less and less like going out again after returning home from work. For simplicity's sake, I got into the habit of making dinner using samples of my products that I would store in my home refrigerator. After describing and selling these products all day, I began to cook and experiment with them in the evening, taking a sample cup of my roasted tomatoes, for example, and a cup of artichoke quarters and sautéing them with shrimp or tossing them with freshly cooked pasta. Within minutes I had a fast, inexpensive meal that was delicious and nutritious. Or I'd stuff a chicken with any number of the preserved vegetables in my refrigerator and bake it for an hour. The result: a flavorful main dish that took less than 15 minutes of prep time.

As my daughter grew, it was clear to me that she loved the MedBar products and would eagerly reach for them on the table. It was exactly what I saw in Italy! Children there don't eat "children's" food, they eat what's on the table. I now have two children and a home where MedBar eating is central. The simplicity of this food, and the fact that it's delicious and natural, makes it a favorite for all. I hope you enjoy these recipes as much as my family does.

Introducing the Ingredients

The most surprising and little-known fact about MedBar products is that they combine to make a perfect marinade for cooking. Most of the olives are immersed in a brine/vinegar combination, and the preserved vegetables in oil—primarily a blend of canola/extra virgin olive oil. They pair together as the ideal sauce for sautéing, basting, or simply tossing with greens.

If you think you don't like olives, give naturally cured olives a chance—they are delicious! Most of us in the U.S. grew up eating chemically treated, canned olives that tainted our perception of their true flavor. The olive is a member of the fruit family, and the crop is harvested once a year. All olives are green in color at first and darken to black the longer they stay on the tree. When olives are picked, you can either press them to produce oil or cure them by immersing them in salt water.

The vegetables on the Mediterranean bar hail from around the world; once harvested, they are quickly cleaned, then grilled or roasted, marinated, freshly preserved, and shipped to your market.

The MedBar Approach to Cooking

Without making too many assumptions, I'm writing this book with a few things in mind.

First, I believe that you already know how to cook. You know how to clean and bake a chicken, grill a steak, throw together a pasta. You know the basics, and most likely more. Are you nodding your head? Great, we are on the same page.

Second, you have plenty of your own recipes. You have well-tested dishes from your mother, father, closest friend, and favorite magazines. You've perfected a core group of these, and now they are your go-to recipes—those that you, well, go to when you need to get a meal right.

Third, you have your own style. You cook the way you cook—I'm not going to ask you to change. If you measure with a spoon or a shake, it works.

Fourth, you want new ideas and inspiration. Cooking and creativity work together. Sometimes it takes a picture to spark a new meal.

Finally—and this is for most of us—you like saving time. No need to elaborate further.

RECYCLING

We love, love, love to recycle. In our home, recycling means more than saving bottles and paper bags—it refers to the second bonus meal that we often enjoy the day after preparing a MedBar dish, using leftovers.

Cooking anything takes time and effort, so we tend to make more than we need. This pays off in extra portions of simple meals that are even easier to assemble than they were the first time. Throughout this book, you'll see ideas for recycling leftovers.

One of our absolute favorites? Recycling extra cooked whole chicken into tasty soft tacos.

PANTRY ESSENTIALS

- ☐ Sea salt
- ☐ Peppercorns
- ☐ Fresh garlic
- ☐ Herbs: basil, thyme, oregano
- ☐ Spices: paprika, espelette, mustard
- ☐ Hot sauce
- ☐ Balsamic vinegar
- ☐ Extra-virgin olive oil
- ☐ Brown sugar
- ☐ Flour

My Basic Techniques

Pizza Dough

House Rule: Buy it! We love having pizza dough around. Aside from my nephew, Gabriel, I've never encountered anyone who doesn't love pizza. It's traditional, versatile, and a crowd-pleaser.

Years ago, we used to make our own pizza dough. We played around with different flours and yeasts, even adding fancy water. It would take a bit of time, make a bit of a mess, but ultimately be delicious. And then I stumbled across a great idea…buying dough from a local pizzeria. Pizzerias make dough for a living—their dough is consistent, available, and generally affordable: A ball of dough big enough for one pizza should cost no more than a dollar or two, and most establishments are happy to sell you their product. It saves time and avoids the mess without any downside.

Pizza dough is ideally rolled out on a smooth, cold surface, like a marble slab. I like to use a French rolling pin, a wooden bread-baker's tool that lets me apply pressure in very specific places. Flour goes on your hands, on your board, and on your pin. The flour prevents the dough from sticking, which can lead to a tear or hole. Olive oil helps if the dough gets too dry. Use a little bit at a time, and your dough will become more flexible. You can roll pizza dough thick or thin, as a circle, a half-moon, or a narrow rectangle. Any way you go, pizza is a great canvas.

Cooking with Hobo Pouches

House Rule: Essential. I consider aluminum foil a real go-to. It's flexible, very easy to cook with, and makes cleanup incredibly easy. I use foil frequently to build a "hobo pouch." It's a simple concept: Place your ingredients in the center of a large sheet of foil, then bring the ends together and fold them over tightly to create a small pouch. I usually double up two sheets of foil, about 15" long, for a stronger seal.

By leaving a little space in the top of the pouch, you help the ingredients to steam in their marinade or oil and cook together beautifully. You can throw hobo pouches directly onto a grill or in the oven. Make sure to always keep your pouch upright to prevent spillage.

Grilling

House Rule: If you have access to a grill, use it. I love food off the grill. It's a very interactive way of cooking, really gets people excited, and results in amazing tastes.

When grilling, we primarily use a technique called indirect grilling, which relies on circulating heat to cook rather than direct heat. By removing direct heat, flare-ups and burning risk are reduced. For chicken or meats, indirect heat allows you to slowly render the fat out of what you are cooking. This gives you crispy skin on chicken, and a nice crust on ribs—in both cases with much less fat than you'd think.

Grilling and indoor cooking have much in common. A convection oven follows the same principles of indirect grilling. This allows our recipes to transfer indoors and out, depending on the season.

Pasta

House Rules: Read the box! We cook pasta nearly every day. Pasta manufacturers know how to cook their product, so I always follow their instructions on cooking time. Taste the pasta toward the end of the indicated time. If you like it a little more al dente (firmer), drain it early. If you like it softer, let it ride.

After I drain the pasta, I return it to the original pan with some remaining pasta water. This will keep it moist and prevent the pasta from sticking together while you assemble the topping or sauce.

Pasta has great resilience: I tend to make more than I need, cooking it to just firm, and storing the leftovers in the fridge. This comes in handy when the kids are hungry RIGHT NOW and you just need to get something on the table. Dump the cold pasta into a pot, add some very hot water, stir a couple of minutes, and your pasta is good to go!

13

Starters

The dishes in this section are ideal for warming up the palate, but they offer more than just a prelude to the main course — they also hold up on their own as mini-meals, or on a snack table when combined. I've found them to be particularly indispensable on those weekend afternoons when my family is hungry but dinner is still hours away. And because these recipes are both easy to make and fun to eat, they shine at last-minute cocktail parties or other spontaneous gatherings.

Olive and Cheese Plate

Castelvetrano:
mild and buttery.

French Cocktail Mix:
a combination of young
(green) and mature (black)
olives prepared with herbs and
lupini beans (a high-protein
sister bean to the edamame).

Kalamata:
deep-flavored and red-winey.

Because MedBar flavors are selected to work in concert with each other, you can choose almost any combination from the bar and serve it on a cheese and cracker plate.

Still, there are specific MedBar combinations that seem destined for each other. I like to group olives of assorted colors and various regions together. The platter on the right includes green Castelvetrano olives from Sicily, a French cocktail mix from the south of France, and Kalamatas from the Peloponnese region of Greece.

You can serve these olives with soft, medium, and firm cheeses from different parts of the world, and/or from different animals: goat, cow, and sheep.

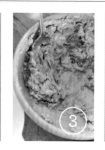
18

Shrimp and Avocado Toasts

1. In a hot pan coated with olive oil, sauté shrimp until pink, about 3 minutes each side. Remove shrimp and set aside, keeping the hot oil in the pan.

2. Using the same pan, sauté a single layer of baguette slices in the leftover olive oil until golden brown. Set aside.

3. In a bowl, mash avocado with a fork.

4. Butterfly shrimp by cutting down the center and opening flat, removing tail.

5. Place a dollop of avocado on each slice of bread. Add roasted garlic and roasted tomato bruschetta to taste.

6. Lay shrimp across bruschetta and finish with a piece of roasted red tomato on top. Sprinkle with sea salt and a squeeze of fresh lemon.

TIP

This is the ultimate cocktail party snack: small but substantial.

scoop Kalamata olives
(pitted)

scoop roasted
red tomatoes

scoop marinated
artichoke quarters

scoop gigandes beans

---

from the pantry
olive oil

---

shopping list
fresh baguette

Antipasti Toasts

1. Chop all MedBar ingredients into small chunks.

2. Slice baguette into thin pieces, about 1/3-inch thick.

3. In a hot pan lined with olive oil, toast the bread until browned: about 2 minutes each side.

4. Spoon chopped ingredients on top of warm bread.

TIP

These toasts pair well with a crisp white wine.

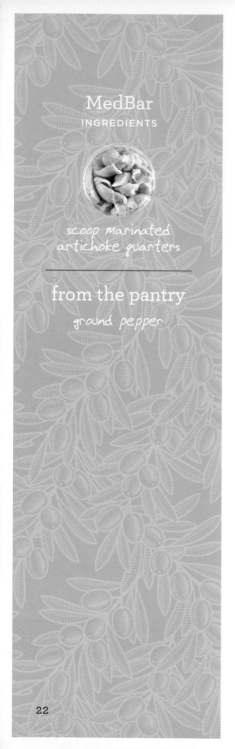
scoop marinated
artichoke quarters

from the pantry

ground pepper

Crispy Artichoke Chips

1. Pull apart artichoke quarters into individual leaves and lay out on a baking sheet.

2. Drizzle the artichoke brine over leaves. Season with ground pepper to your liking.

3. Bake in a preheated oven at 375°F for 20 minutes.

🌸 **TIP**

The crunch of these chips makes them a great alternative to the potato variety.

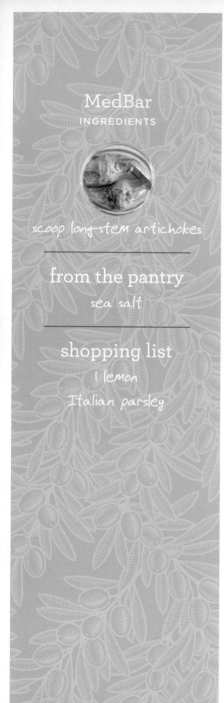

MedBar
INGREDIENTS

scoop long-stem artichokes

---

from the pantry
sea salt

---

shopping list
I lemon

Italian parsley

Simple Grilled Artichokes

1. Slice long-stem artichokes in half lengthwise.

2. Place halves on a heated grill so they lie flat.

3. When crispy and caramelized, flip artichokes.

4. Squeeze lemon over the top, and sprinkle with sea salt and parsley.

TIP

These artichokes also make for a tasty brunch when prepared with fried or scrambled eggs.

scoop cipolline onions
(sliced)

scoop Peppadew

shopping list

flour tortillas

slices of cheddar
or Jack cheese

Sweet and Spicy Quesadilla

(1) In a hot pan, sauté the Peppadew, including up to $1/4$ cup of the sweet and spicy Peppadew sauce.

(2) Stir in sliced cipolline onions with their balsamic vinegar.

(3) Simmer for 3 minutes. Set aside and wipe down pan.

(4) Place a tortilla in the hot pan, topping it with two slices of cheddar or Jack cheese.

(5) Spread the Peppadew and onions over cheese.

(6) Top with a second tortilla and cook for 2 minutes. Flip quesadilla, letting the second side cook for 2 minutes.

(7) Flip and press quickly; repeat. Remove and quarter.

TIP

For a kick, add a little of your favorite hot sauce.

Mushroom and Tomato Quesadilla

shopping list

flour tortillas

slices of cheddar
or Jack cheese

(1) Chop up the marinated mushrooms and roasted tomatoes.

(2) In a hot pan, sauté mushrooms and tomatoes for 3 to 4 minutes. Set aside and wipe down pan.

(3) Place a tortilla in the pan and top with two slices of cheddar or Jack cheese.

(4) Spread mushrooms and tomatoes over the cheese. Top with a second tortilla and cook for 2 minutes.

(5) Flip quesadilla and let the other side cook for 2 minutes.

(6) Flip and press quickly; repeat. Remove and quarter.

TIP

For smaller appetites, simply halve the ingredients and instead of adding a second tortilla, fold tortilla over into a half-moon.

Salads & Sides

Though I'm a big fan of one-pot meals that sensibly combine the main protein with a supporting grain or veggie (along with fewer pans to wash), I also enjoy the presentational charm of serving individual side dishes, particularly when entertaining. I think you'll find that these stellar sides and salads will enliven the center of your table and complement any entrée, all with minimal effort.

Fresh Corn Bruschetta Salad

1 Cook whole ears of corn for 5 to 7 minutes in boiling water; drain. When cool enough to handle, slice kernels off the cob.

2 Put corn kernels in a bowl and scoop roasted tomato bruschetta on top, ideally in a 1:1 ratio.

3 Mix well, adding a pinch each of salt and pepper.

TIP

For an even quicker preparation, or if fresh corn is out of season, use frozen corn thawed to room temperature.

from the pantry

sea salt

ground pepper

shopping list

bag of preferred mixed lettuce

8oz ball of fresh mozzarella

European Salad

1. Empty mixed lettuce into a bowl.

2. Add scoop of roasted tomatoes to the lettuce, including marinade.

3. Slice mozzarella to your liking and add to bowl. Add your preferred olives, including 5 or 6 tablespoons of brine.

4. Toss ingredients; sprinkle with salt and pepper.

✺ TIP

Olives come in their own distinctive brines and oils. Rebalance your salad to taste with balsamic vinegar or olive oil.

scoop gigandes beans

scoop roasted
red tomatoes

---

shopping list

head of butter lettuce

1 red onion

Spring Salad

(1) Clean and pull apart head of lettuce; pat dry.

(2) In a salad bowl, tear lettuce leaves into desired size.

(3) Slice the red onion as thinly as you can and add to lettuce.

(4) Add gigandes beans and roasted tomatoes to the bowl, including all their juices.

(5) Toss and serve.

TIP

The marinade from the beans and tomatoes serves as ample dressing, but if you prefer more tartness, squeeze a fresh lemon over salad before tossing.

MedBar
INGREDIENTS

scoop Kalamata
olives (pitted)

scoop roasted
red tomatoes

scoop gigandes beans
in vinaigrette

from the pantry

sea salt

shopping list

romaine lettuce

1 red onion

Mediterranean Salad

1   Clean and pull apart lettuce leaves; pat dry.

2   Using your hands, tear lettuce into bite-sized pieces in a salad bowl. Dice red onion and scatter on lettuce.

3   Scoop all MedBar ingredients into the bowl, including all their oil and brine. Sprinkle with salt, toss, and serve!

TIP

If you have the time, chop this salad into fine pieces and serve with an ice cream scooper next to your center-of-the-plate protein.

Baked Artichoke Parmesan

1. Scoop marinated artichokes into a baking dish.

2. Sprinkle generously with shaved or grated Parmesan.

3. Bake in a preheated oven at 400°F for 20 minutes.

TIP

Individual earthenware baking cups, or ramekins, are ideal for this dish.

Cheesy Asparagus

1. Spoon the asparagus salad, including a splash of its brine, into an individual crock (use one scoop of asparagus per one-serving crock).

2. Place a slice of cheddar cheese over asparagus (presliced squares are great if you're short on time).

3. Bake in a preheated oven at 350°F for 20 minutes.

TIP
This is one of my go-to family side dishes, as it meets all of my requirements: easy, healthy, delicious, and kid-friendly.

MedBar
INGREDIENTS

scoop Kalamata olives
(pitted)

shopping list
feta cheese

Baked Kalamata with Feta

1. Slice pitted Kalamata olives into halves and place in a small baking dish.

2. Slice or break feta cheese into small chunks and scatter over olives.

3. Bake in a preheated oven at 350°F for 20 minutes.

🌸 TIP

If you only have whole, unpitted olives, you can pit them by placing the flat side of a chef's knife over each olive. Apply pressure downward on the knife until the olive flesh breaks away from the pit. Pull flesh in half and remove pit.

MedBar
INGREDIENTS

scoop roasted tomato bruschetta

scoop mushroom bruschetta

shopping list

shaved or grated Parmesan cheese

46

Baked Bruschetta

1. Scoop the mushroom bruschetta into a small baking dish. Top with roasted tomato bruschetta.

2. Sprinkle generously with Parmesan.

3. Bake in a preheated oven at 350°F for 20 minutes.

TIP

For an easy finger snack or appetizer, spoon contents of the baking dish onto slices of grilled bread.

Pizza & Pasta

My cooking may have evolved over the years, but my devotion to the simplicity and honesty of Italian food is unwavering. The pages in this section are borne out of years of pizza, pasta, and stromboli worship, with most of these recipes seeing frequent rotation on our family table. To this day I could easily eat pizza and pasta every day, and the truth is, I often do.

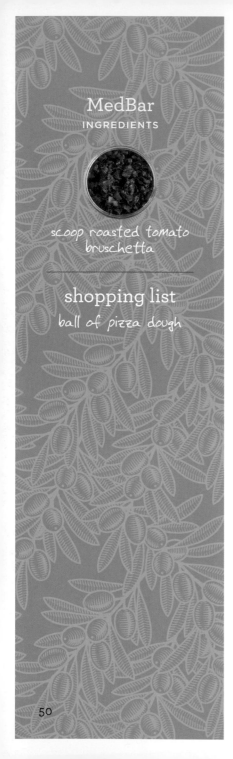

MedBar
INGREDIENTS

scoop roasted tomato bruschetta

shopping list
ball of pizza dough

Roasted Tomato Bruschetta Pizza

(1)

(2)

(3)

(1) Place rolled-out pizza dough on a baking sheet or earthenware pan.

(2) Scoop the roasted tomato bruschetta onto dough, spreading it to the edges.

(3) Bake in a preheated oven at 450°F for 12 to 15 minutes.

TIP

Who says pizza has to come in a perfect circle? Pressing your dough into an irregular shape gives your pie an artisanal feel.

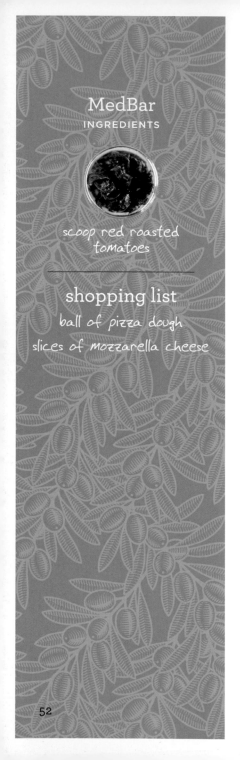

Roasted Tomato and Mozzarella Pizza

(1) Place rolled-out pizza dough on a baking pan and drizzle with oil marinade from the roasted tomatoes.

(2) Use a spoon to spread oil evenly until dough is covered and moist (not soaked).

(3) Place slices of mozzarella on the dough, about a half-inch apart.

(4) Scatter roasted tomatoes over dough.

(5) Bake in a preheated oven at 450°F for 12 to 15 minutes.

 TIP

You can avoid burning the crust by dabbing olive oil on any dry, uncovered dough before baking. (See image #4.)

MedBar
INGREDIENTS

scoop *Kalamata olives (pitted)*

scoop *Castelvetrano olives (pitted)*

from the pantry

olive oil

shopping list

ball of pizza dough

shaved or grated Parmesan cheese

Two Olives Pizza

(1) Slice pitted Kalamata and Castelvetrano olives into halves.

(2) Place rolled-out pizza dough on a cutting board, baking sheet, or earthenware pan and drizzle with olive oil.

(3) Use a spoon to spread oil evenly until dough is moist (not soaked).

(4) Arrange olives over dough so that halves are just touching. Sprinkle with shaved or grated Parmesan.

(5) Bake in a preheated oven at 450°F for 12 to 15 minutes.

❧ TIP

For extra Mediterranean flavor, serve this pizza with a side of hummus.

MedBar
INGREDIENTS

scoop roasted tomato
bruschetta

shopping list
fresh mozzarella sheet
ball of pizza dough

Playtime Pizza

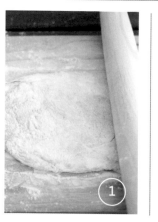   

1. Roll out pizza dough.

2. Unroll fresh mozzarella sheet and use cookie cutters to create shapes.

3. Spread tomato bruschetta over dough.

4. Top with mozzarella shapes.

5. Bake in preheated oven at 450°F for 12 to 15 minutes.

TIP

Adding playful shapes to pizza not only makes cooking fun for kids, it also disarms picky eaters.

Cheeseburger Stromboli

   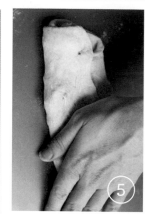

1. In a hot pan with olive oil, sauté ground beef until browned.

2. Stir in roasted red tomatoes and sliced cipolline onions, including the juices they came with.

3. After rolling out pizza dough, cut it in half. Place one semicircle on a baking sheet or earthenware dish.

4. Spread center of dough with the beef filling, topping with two slices of cheddar. Drizzle with olive oil.

5. Fold dough over the filling, overlapping edges much like you would wrap a present. Close any gaps by pinching dough.

6. Bake in a preheated oven at 375°F for 30 minutes.

7. Once baked, drizzle olive oil over the crust and slice your stromboli in half.

❧ TIP

Because pizza and strombolis are cousins, any pizza topping will work well as a stromboli filling.

MedBar

INGREDIENTS

scoop Kalamata
olives (pitted)

from the pantry

olive oil

shopping list

3 lamb sausages,
casings removed

ball of pizza dough

feta cheese

Greek-Style Lamb Stromboli

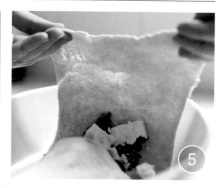

(1) In a hot pan, sauté the lamb sausage until browned.

(2) Stir pitted Kalamata olives into pan with lamb, including up to $1/4$ cup of the brine. Chop warmed olives with the end of your wooden spoon.

(3) Roll out dough and place on a baking sheet or earthenware pan. Spread lamb and olives down the center.

(4) Top with chunks of feta cheese.

(5) Fold dough over filling, creating an enclosed pouch by overlapping and pinching dough edges.

(6) Drizzle olive oil over stromboli and bake in a preheated oven at 375°F for 30 minutes.

🌸 TIP

For more Greek flavor, serve this stromboli with tzatziki or Greek yogurt.

Mozza-Peppa Stromboli

(1) In a hot pan, sauté the sausage until browned.

(2) Stir Peppadew into the pan, including up to ¼ cup of the marinade.

(3) Roll out dough and place on a baking sheet or earthenware pan. Spread sausage filling down the center.

(4) Follow with wedges of mozzarella.

(5) Fold dough over filling, overlapping and pinching edges to create an enclosed pouch.

(6) Bake in a preheated oven at 350°F for 20 minutes.

(7) Remove stromboli from oven and fully cover with your favorite marinara sauce. Return to oven for an additional 10 to 12 minutes.

⚜ TIP

Have some stromboli filling left over? You can save it to mix with marinara sauce for your next pasta dinner.

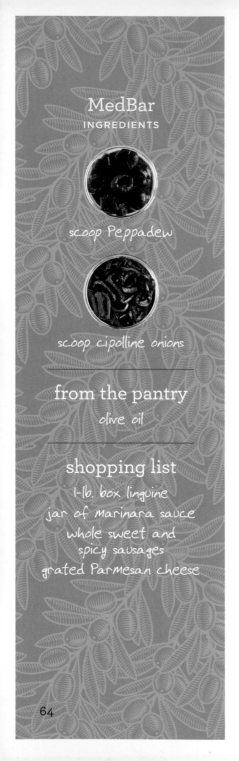

MedBar
INGREDIENTS

scoop Peppadew

scoop cipolline onions

from the pantry

olive oil

shopping list

1-lb. box linguine
jar of marinara sauce
whole sweet and
spicy sausages
grated Parmesan cheese

Sweet and Spicy Sausage Marinara

 ①  ②  ③  ⑤  ⑥

① Scatter the Peppadew and cipolline onions in a baking dish (preferably glass or ceramic), and lay sausages on top.

② Drizzle olive oil over baking dish in the shape of a large *S*.

③ Bake uncovered in a preheated oven at 325°F for 30 to 35 minutes. Remove from oven and chop sausages into bite-sized pieces.

④ Boil your preferred pasta as directed on the box (linguine is particularly excellent with this dish).

⑤ Warm your favorite marinara sauce for 4 to 5 minutes and pour over sausage mix. (Or try your supermarket's own house-label sauce—I'm certain it's excellent!)

⑥ Toss sausages, vegetables, and sauce with the cooked pasta. Sprinkle with Parmesan.

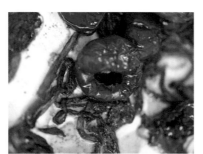

🎗 TIP

During the baking period, I love the way the cipolline onions and Peppadew crust and caramelize. Be sure to scrape the pan so the sweet, crunchy parts make their way into the sauce.

MedBar
INGREDIENTS

scoop roasted garlic

---

shopping list

1-lb. box linguine

6 slices of bacon or pancetta

shaved or grated Parmesan cheese

Linguine Carbonara

1. Boil linguine as directed on the box.

2. Chop the roasted garlic.

3. Pan-fry slices of bacon or pancetta over a medium flame for 8 to 10 minutes, flipping halfway.

4. Chop the bacon slices; return bacon to pan and sauté with the garlic over a medium flame.

5. Toss cooked pasta with simmering bacon and garlic.

6. Sprinkle generously with Parmesan and serve.

❦ TIP

Traditional carbonaras use egg yolks, which can make the recipe more complicated and less healthy. This version is much lighter, saves several steps, and is equally delicious.

MedBar
INGREDIENTS

scoop mushroom bruschetta

scoop roasted garlic

scoop roasted red peppers

---

from the pantry

splash of white wine or chicken stock

---

shopping list

2 dozen Manila clams

1-lb. box of your preferred pasta

Roasted Ragu with Manila Clams

1. Clean the Manila clams and set aside in refrigerator.

2. Boil the pasta of your choice as directed on the box (this dish can handle a wider pasta).

3. Chop the roasted garlic and roasted red peppers.

4. Scoop the mushroom bruschetta into a hot pan and stir.

5. After a minute or so, add the garlic and peppers. Add a splash of white wine or stock. Lower flame and let ragu simmer.

6. Place clams over ragu and simmer until clams pop open. Discard any unopened clams.

7. Pour the clam ragu over cooked pasta and serve.

TIP
Soak your clams in a mixture of cold water and cornmeal for 30 minutes before cooking; this will help release excess sand.

Spicy Shrimp in Angel Hair

scoop roasted tomato bruschetta

---

from the pantry
hot pepper flakes

---

shopping list
1 dozen whole shrimp, cleaned and deveined

1-lb. box angel hair pasta

shaved or grated Parmesan cheese

(1) Over a low flame, spread a half-scoop of roasted tomato bruschetta into a pan (you'll use the other half shortly).

(2) Place shrimp in the bubbling bruschetta. Flip shrimp as they turn pink, cooking 2 to 3 minutes each side.

(3) Boil angel hair as directed on the box.

(4) Scoop the remaining tomato bruschetta onto shrimp. Stir and flip shrimp over. Turn off flame.

(5) Toss cooked pasta with shrimp and bruschetta.

(6) Sprinkle with hot pepper flakes to taste. Top with Parmesan if desired.

✿ TIP

I keep a bag of clean, deveined shrimp in my freezer at all times. It's an instant meal-maker when you don't have the time or energy to shop for dinner.

Double-Roasted Vegetable Pasta

① Boil rigatoni as directed on the box.

② In a hot pan, sauté the red and yellow peppers for 3 to 4 minutes.

③ Add roasted tomatoes and half a jar of marinara sauce to pan. Stir.

④ Pour sauce over cooked rigatoni.

⑤ Sprinkle with freshly shaved or grated Parmesan.

❦ TIP

Did you know this dish easily transforms into baked "ziti"? Just top with mozzarella and bake in oven for 10 minutes or so until cheese melts.

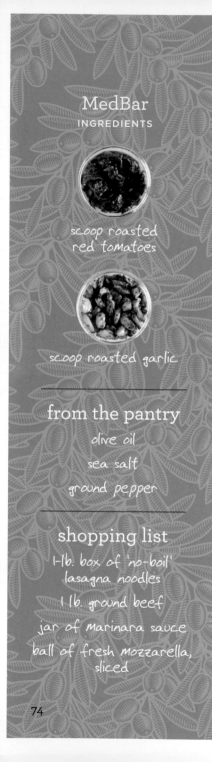
Double-Helping Lasagna

1. In a hot pan, sauté about one pound of ground beef until browned. Add salt and pepper to your liking.

2. Stir one-quarter jar of your favorite marinara sauce into the pan with beef (you'll use the rest in the coming steps). Stir and simmer for 3 to 4 minutes.

3. Spread a scoop of the meat sauce onto the base of a baking dish and lay no-boil lasagna noodles over the top. The strips should overlap slightly. Spread another scoop of sauce over the noodles.

4. Scatter a small scoop of roasted tomatoes over the top, including their oil marinade. Layer again with noodles, sauce, and mozzarella.

5. Continue layering with both beef and marinara sauces, roasted garlic, tomatoes, cheese, and noodles. Finish with a layer of mozzarella.

6. Cover dish with foil and bake in a preheated oven at 375°F for 45 minutes. Uncover and return to oven for 5 to 10 minutes until cheese is melted.

✿ TIP

I like to double this recipe and freeze the extra lasagna for a future meal.

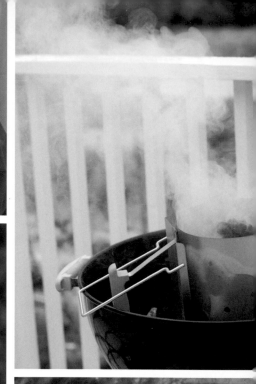

Entrées

Having prepared and presented hundreds of recipes, I elected to include only those that were simple, delicious, and consistent winners. My home is my test kitchen, and making meals that my children will eat and enjoy is my priority. This section features the evening crowd-pleasers that I enjoy making, love eating, and adore seeing others devour.

MedBar
INGREDIENTS

scoop artichoke quarters

scoop gigandes beans

from the pantry
olive oil · sea salt

shopping list
half a chicken

78

Chicken Baked with Gigandes and Artichokes

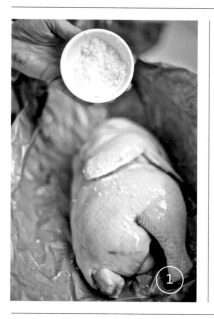  

(1) Rinse chicken, pat dry, and coat skin with olive oil. Rub with salt to taste and place in a casserole dish.

(2) Empty a generous scoop of gigandes beans over chicken, including the marinade.

(3) Follow with a generous scoop of artichoke quarters and their marinade. Bake in a preheated oven at 375°F for 50 minutes.

 TIP

This recipe also works well with mixed chicken parts, especially thighs.

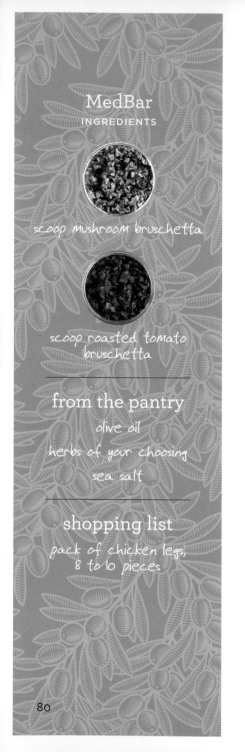
Easiest Chicken Legs Ever

(1) Empty both scoops of bruschetta into a searing hot skillet.

(2) Stir bruschettas for 3 to 4 minutes, releasing their juices.

(3) Arrange cleaned chicken legs in the skillet. Drizzle with olive oil, and sprinkle with salt and the herbs of your choosing. Place entire skillet in a preheated oven and bake at 375°F for 40 minutes.

✾ TIP

After removing the legs, be sure to scoop all of the crispy bits from the bottom of the pan to sprinkle on top for a tasty, crunchy treat.

MedBar
INGREDIENTS

scoop gigandes beans
in vinaigrette

scoop roasted garlic

scoop mushroom bruschetta

scoop marinated mushrooms

from the pantry
olive oil · sea salt · pepper

shopping list
1 whole chicken

Ultimate Stuffed Chicken

(1) Rinse chicken inside and out, pat dry, and coat skin with olive oil. Rub with salt and pepper to taste.

(2) Scoop about half of each portion of MedBar vegetables, including their juices, into chicken cavity.

(3) Place stuffed chicken in an earthenware dish or roasting pan. Drizzle olive oil and vegetable juices over chicken and scatter remaining gigandes beans, garlic, and mushrooms in the pan. Bake in a preheated oven at 375°F for about an hour.

(4) Remove chicken and cut into rough pieces. Serve on platter surrounded with cooked vegetables and juices.

 TIP

I love to recycle remaining chicken and MedBar vegetables the next day by making soft tacos.

Pork 'n' Gigandes Beans

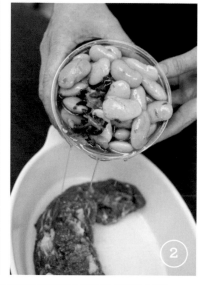

(1) Clean and salt the pork loin. Lay in a baking dish.

(2) Empty a generous scoop of gigandes beans into the dish, including the oil. Rub oil over pork loin so that it's completely covered; this will help it caramelize in the oven.

(3) Bake in a preheated oven at 425°F for 30 minutes.

🌸 TIP

The classic combo of pork and beans really makes this dish, but if you're feeling adventurous, you can switch out the pork loin for chops or even baby back ribs.

Jumbo Shrimp with Gigandes and Feta

(1) Empty gigandes beans into a baking pan (ideally ceramic) and place in oven at 375°F for 12 minutes.

(2) Rinse shrimp and drop in boiling water for 3 to 4 minutes, until pink and cooked through.

(3) Chop boiled shrimp into $1/2$-inch pieces.

(4) Remove gigandes from oven and spoon onto a plate or into a bowl.

(5) Top with shrimp.

(6) Crumble feta over top, garnish with parsley, and finish with olive oil.

❧ TIP

For extra melted deliciousness, add everything to a baking dish and place under your broiler for a few minutes. This will melt the feta to perfection.

scoop Kalamata
olives (pitted)

scoop roasted
red tomatoes

1/4 scoop roasted garlic

from the pantry

1/4 cup white wine or
chicken stock

shopping list

1 whole fish (cleaned
and gutted), preferably
striped bass, red snapper,
or porgy

1 lemon

Stuffed Whole Fish

(1)

(4)

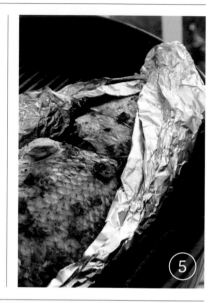

(5)

1. Chop the Kalamata olives, roasted tomatoes, and garlic.

2. Lay cleaned fish on a piece of foil; sprinkle salt and fresh-squeezed lemon juice on top and inside fish.

3. Stuff the fish with chopped ingredients.

4. Scatter remaining MedBar ingredients over the top, turning up the edges of the foil to catch juices.

5. Pour 1/4 cup white wine or chicken stock around fish. Grill or bake in a preheated oven at 375°F for 25 minutes.

✿ TIP

Our beloved nanny, Carol, taught me her secret to cooking whole fish: Use excess liquid so that you're steaming, rather than cooking the fish directly. Maximize steam by making a pouch around the fish with the foil.

MedBar
INGREDIENTS

scoop roasted
red peppers

scoop cipolline onions

---

from the pantry

olive oil

---

shopping list

4 chicken sausage links
(precooked)

ball of fresh mozzarella

fresh baguette

jar of marinara sauce

Sausage Grinder

1. Chop roasted red peppers and cipolline onions.

2. Slice fresh mozzarella.

3. Sauté sausages over a medium flame for about 4 minutes, rotating regularly. They should be hot and crispy.

4. Slice sausages into coins; return to pan with red peppers and onions. Sauté.

5. Assemble grinder: On a sliced baguette drizzled with olive oil, add sausage mixture, marinara, and mozzarella slices.

6. Bake in a preheated oven at 375°F for about 15 minutes, until cheese is bubbling.

❧ TIP

If you like your grinder on the goopy side, add more marinara sauce before baking.

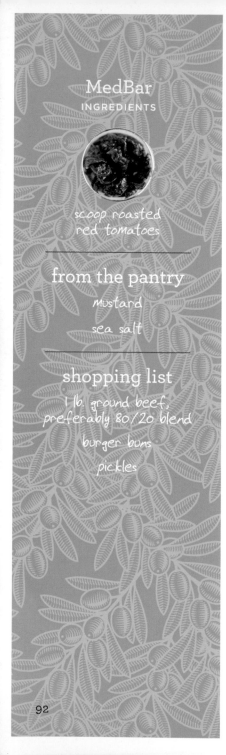
MedBar Burger

1. Place ground beef in a bowl; add a squirt of mustard and pinch of salt.

2. Mix beef and shape into round patties. Place on grill.

3. Grill patties to desired doneness; flip.

4. Place roasted tomatoes directly onto grill, cooking until sizzling and crispy.

5. Toss buns onto grill, removing when browned.

6. Finish burger with grilled tomatoes and a side of pickles.

🌿 TIP

Most MedBar ingredients make great burger toppings. Try roasted tomato bruschetta, mushroom bruschetta, or cipolline onions. For a softer, juicier texture, add any of these to a hobo pouch and grill or bake for 5 to 7 minutes.

MedBar Product Guide

Castelvetrano olives

 TASTING NOTE: I often refer to these perfectly round, bright green olives as the perfect "starter" olive. They are mild and delicious and impossible to dislike. If you close your eyes and taste, all you feel and think is butter, butter, butter!

ORIGIN: Sicily, Italy

Also available whole (with pit) or pitted (without pit)

Kalamata olives

TASTING NOTE: I am constantly amazed at how much Americans love the Kalamata olive. Perhaps it's their purple hue and distinct pointy tip that initially attracts. Or their deep red-wine flavor? Like all wonderful things, Kalamata olives get copied—often sold as "Calamata." A true Kalamata grows in nothern Greece and exudes centuries of mature, black-olive deliciousness. Ideal served as a cheese pairing with red wine or as an ingredient to deliver a spark of saltiness and meaty texture.

ORIGIN: Greece

 Also available whole or pitted

---

olive mixes

TASTING NOTE: Although olives now grow all over the world, Greece and France produce some of the best so-called table olives. Farmers in those countries have been growing and curing olives for centuries and take great pride in what they produce. An ideal "table mix" has green, blond, and black olives of different sizes, and most important, they are cured naturally.

ORIGIN: Greece and France

 Also available whole or pitted

stuffed green olives

TASTING NOTE: In America most people envision stuffed olives with a red pimento center, even though the "pimento" is actually sugar paste and a far cry from the real pepper. Naturally cured green olives hand-stuffed with real ingredients like creamy blue cheese, spicy aji peppers, sweet red peppers, or garlic are special and delicious. For starters, they are beautiful to look at. They stand out on a cheese plate or as a snack during cocktail hour. Start a festive evening with them immersed in a martini or Bloody Mary.

 ORIGIN: Aji-stuffed olive: Peru · red-pepper-stuffed or blue-cheese-stuffed olive: Greece

---

black oil-cured olives

TASTING NOTE: Most smooth-skinned olives are cured in salt water; oil-cured olives have a wrinkled appearance. Oil-cured refers to an olive that has been cured in salt and never immersed in salt water. The oil from the olive releases (hence the name), resulting in an intense, licorice-like flavor.

 ORIGIN: Morocco

 Also available whole or pitted

---

roasted red tomatoes

TASTING NOTE: With their meaty texture and limited seeds, Roma are the ideal roasting tomatoes. I love their versatility, bright red color, and intensely sweet flavor—captured during those few months when tomatoes are at their ripest and brightest. After a slow roasting, the tomatoes are immersed in a flavorful oil marinade that works as a ready-made sauce for virtually any meal.

 ORIGIN: East Coast, U.S.

 Also available seasonally in yellow

---

roasted tomato bruschetta

TASTING NOTE: This bruschetta is a combination of half roasted red tomatoes (above) and half fresh Roma tomatoes, peeled and chopped. Essentially, it's a sweet, roasted, moist tomato base. The flavor of the oil and herbs make it the perfect base for a sauce, topping, or dressing.

 ORIGIN: East Coast, U.S.

Peppadew

 TASTING NOTE: Peppadew are small, round, South African peppers that are hollowed, cleaned, and then immersed in a unique sweet and spicy sauce. Peppadew fall into an unusual category, as they are both a brand and type of pepper. I love eating these alone, stuffed with cheese, or in any number of recipes.

 ORIGIN: South Africa

 Also available in yellow, known as "golden"

roasted red peppers

 TASTING NOTE: Roasted red peppers add a touch of sweetness and a hearty texture to any sauce, sandwich, or pizza. With their bright red color and malleability, strips of roasted peppers can also be layered and arranged as a flavorful, decorative garnish to many dishes.

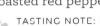 **ORIGIN:** Greece

 Also available thinly sliced ("strips")

marinated mushrooms

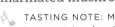 **TASTING NOTE:** Mushrooms have been used for centuries in many styles of cooking, but in my opinion, they taste best marinated in oil with generous amounts of garlic. Aside from the smooth and meaty texture of these button mushrooms, I love their intense garlic flavor. Mushrooms are porous by nature; they absorb the pungent aroma and taste of their garlic marinade, making them perfect for sautéing or simply warming as a vegetable side.

 ORIGIN: East Coast, U.S.

 Also available in teriyaki sauce and finely chopped as mushroom bruschetta

gigandes beans in vinaigrette

 TASTING NOTE: I warn you that when you come across these big, buttery, delicious beans marinating in oil and vinegar, you may not be able to stop eating them! I use gigandes cold in salads or warmed and served with chicken or pork. The mild flavor and meaty texture complement both beautifully.

ORIGIN: Greece

 Also available in tomato sauce

cipolline onions

 TASTING NOTE: Cipolline are small, flat onions that originated in Italy. MedBar cipolline are the Borettane variety, marinated in balsamic vinegar. Every time I taste these sweet, crunchy onions I imagine they must have been marinating for weeks to achieve their incredibly complex and delicious flavor. They pair beautifully served cool with cheese and olives—but they also caramelize perfectly in a baking dish.

 ORIGIN: Italy

 Also available thinly sliced

roasted garlic

 TASTING NOTE: Quality slow-roasted garlic truly enables you to make a delicious meal in minutes, as it can be added to whatever is in your refrigerator. The smoky-sweet flavor and plump texture bring the simplest of foods to life. I use roasted garlic in virtually all of my dishes, but I especially enjoy it on nights when I want the simplest of preparations—say, warmed and tossed with pasta and grated Parmesan . . . mmmm!

ORIGIN: California, U.S.

marinated artichokes

 TASTING NOTE: I believe artichokes are one of the most delicious vegetables on the planet, but they are difficult to prepare at home: Raw artichokes are hard and bristly and require a good deal of work to cut and clean. That's why finding well-made marinated artichokes is so special. The flavor is divine—and they have many recipe applications. Serve them cool in a salad, warm under fish—or, my favorite, tossed with pasta and topped with grated cheese.

 ORIGIN: Peru or Italy

 Also available in quarters (cut into 4 pieces per head), baby hearts (the head), or long-stem (whole artichoke)

grilled asparagus salad

TASTING NOTE: Recalling an asparagus recipe I found in a French cookbook from 1840 reminds me how challenging it was to secure these vegetables centuries ago, and I'm grateful for today's easy access to tender green and white asparagus, charred and immersed in a blend of oil and vinegar. Depending on the time of day and season, I'll toss these with salad greens or broil them under cheddar cheese slices for a decadent yet healthy side dish.

ORIGIN: Peru

To Savannah and Connor, for eating everything.

Thank you to all of the collaborators who helped create this book, specifically Megan McFarland and Dan Tucker of Sideshow Media for their help in shaping our concept. Thanks to Celia Fuller for her remarkable design aesthetic and ability to match the visuals with the vision. Thank you to Nova Jacobs for her insight and careful editing.

Hearty thanks go out to all of the Brennans and Shaubs, and to our friends of all ages who love celebrating life through festive meals.

Thank you to Karen Benvin, my mentor, who twenty years ago promised me a very bright future if I always kept my word and never let a day end without taking at least one order.

Thank you, Phil and Kevin.

And thank you to all of the smart, successful women I admire, learn from, and work with—you know exactly who you are.